CLASSIC CARS
AN IMAGINATION LIBRARY SERIES

THE STORY OF

Chevy Impalas

by David K. Wright

Gareth Stevens Publishing
A WORLD ALMANAC EDUCATION GROUP COMPANY

Please visit our web site at: www.garethstevens.com
For a free color catalog describing Gareth Stevens Publishing's
list of high-quality books and multimedia programs,
call 1-800-542-2595 (USA) or 1-800-387-3178 (Canada).
Gareth Stevens Publishing's fax: (414) 332-3567.

Library of Congress Cataloging-in-Publication Data

Wright, David K.
    The story of Chevy Impalas / by David K. Wright.
       p. cm. — (Classic cars: an imagination library series)
    Includes bibliographical references and index.
    Summary: Surveys the history of this popular Chevrolet, which has enjoyed
enormous popularity as a large, fast, and affordable car from the time it was
introduced in 1958, through the years it when it was not manufactured, and into
its reemergence in 2000.
    ISBN 0-8368-3190-X (lib. bdg.)
    1. Impala automobile—Juvenile literature. [1. Impala automobile—History.]
I. Title.
TL215.I43W75   2002
629.222'2—dc21   2002072396

First published in 2002 by
Gareth Stevens Publishing
A World Almanac Education Group Company
330 West Olive Street, Suite 100
Milwaukee, WI 53212 USA

Text: David K. Wright
Cover design and page layout: Scott M. Krall
Series editor: Jim Mezzanotte
Picture Researcher: Diane Laska-Swanke

Photo credits: Cover, pp. 5, 7, 9, 19, 21 © Ron Kimball; p. 11 © Isaac Hernández/MercuryPress.com;
p. 13 © Eva Hernández/MercuryPress.com; p. 15 © MercuryPress.com; p. 17 © Marco de Bari/MercuryPress.com

Printed in the United States of America

1 2 3 4 5 6 7 8 9 06 05 04 03 02

Front cover: **This 1958 Chevy Impala has a special pink paint job. It looks much different from today's small cars!**

TABLE OF CONTENTS

Words that appear in the glossary are printed in **boldface** type the first time they occur in the text.

THE FIRST IMPALAS

In 1958, Chevrolet introduced a new car called the Impala. It was named for a beautiful African antelope that runs fast and leaps very high. The company wanted people to think of a sleek, pretty animal when they saw the new model.

Chevrolet had created a fun car that appealed to young people. The car was big and roomy, but it did not cost a lot of money. "Chevy" cars had been popular for years, but the Impala became the most popular Chevy ever. In its second year, the Impala outsold all the other Chevy models. The car was a huge hit!

Even sitting next to these airplanes, this 1958 "Chevy" Impala looks big! It has a lot of shiny chrome, which was popular at the time.

THE SUPER SPORT

Although Impalas were big and comfortable, many people wanted them to be faster. So in the 1960s, Chevrolet began selling a very fast Impala called the Super Sport. This "muscle car" had a big engine that produced a lot of **horsepower**. The engine also used a lot of gasoline, but at the time, gas was cheap.

Many young adults could afford to own and drive Impalas. On warm summer nights, young people all across the country drove their Impalas to drive-in restaurants and drive-in movie theaters. Cars had become a big part of life in the United States.

*This 1962 Super Sport **convertible** is very fast, but its big engine uses a lot of gas! It would be fun to ride in this car on a warm summer night.*

BIGGER AND BETTER

In 1965, the Chevy Impala set a record for the number of models sold in one year. That year, more than a million Impalas were sold! The Impala's sales were higher than any other single model made by an American car company.

To keep people interested in the Impala, Chevrolet changed the look of the car every year. No matter what changes were made, though, Impalas continued to be big cars, and they used a lot of gas. Gasoline was still cheap, so most people did not care. Impala owners could not understand why anyone would rather drive a little foreign car!

By 1965, the Impala was one of the most popular cars in the United States. This impala is from 1966. It has special wheels and a special paint job.

HIGH-PERFORMANCE IMPALAS

Many people raced Impalas at **drag strips**. The cars did well because they could **accelerate** quickly. Parts for Chevys cost less than parts for other cars, and owners could buy parts that made the Impalas even faster.

Impalas became even more popular when they won races. A lot of people made changes to their Impalas, giving the cars fancy paint jobs or adding special wheels. The Beach Boys recorded a song called "409" about a certain Impala engine that was very powerful. The song became a big hit!

In the 1960s, many Chevy Impalas packed quite a punch under the hood! The owner of this Impala has taken good care of the big engine.

THE LAST CONVERTIBLE

Chevrolet sold many different kinds of Impalas. People could buy them as two-door **convertibles** or **hardtops**, four-door **sedans**, and station wagons.

In 1972, Chevrolet stopped making Impala convertibles. People were more concerned about safety, and they worried about getting hurt if the convertible rolled over. **Insurance** for convertibles also cost more than for other kinds of cars.

The Chevy Impala was still very popular. In 1972, total sales of the Impala reached ten million! That year, the Impala measured over 18 feet (5 meters) long. It was the biggest Impala yet! The car was longer and wider than any Chevy before it.

Convertibles can be a lot of fun, but they can also be very dangerous! A convertible has no hard top to protect people in case of a rollover.

SMALLER IMPALAS

In 1973, the price of gasoline began to rise. Now people wanted cars that used less gas. Chevrolet began to make smaller Impalas that weighed less. Some people missed the huge Impalas of the past, but these new, smaller cars burned less fuel.

Chevrolet stopped making Impalas after 1986, but in 1994, the company once again made an Impala. It was a big, fast Super Sport model. In 1996, Chevrolet decided to stop making the car. Would the company ever make Impalas again?

Like older Impalas, Chevy Impalas from the 1990s were big cars. This four-door Impala is from 1994. Two years later, the cars were no longer made.

IMPALAS IN CUBA

In the United States, people often buy a new car every few years. In many other countries, however, people do not have much money, and they cannot afford to keep buying new cars. When they buy a car, they make it last for a long time!

Over the years, people in other countries have bought Impalas. They still drive their Impalas, using them as family cars and taxis. They also use the cars to **haul** things around.

Many old Impalas can be seen in Cuba, an island in the **Caribbean Sea**. When people in Cuba need parts for their Impalas, they often make them at home. Impalas in Cuba are over forty years old!

This Impala is being driven in Cuba. It is from the 1950s! In Cuba, people keep their old Impalas running, even if it means making parts themselves.

CUSTOM IMPALAS

Today, many young people in the United States like the looks of older Impalas. Some **restore** the cars to their original condition, but others turn their Impalas into **custom** cars that attract a lot of attention!

These Impalas are called "lowriders" because they are very low to the ground. They often have hidden lights, fancy wheels and paint jobs, steering wheels made of chains, and fuzzy, brightly colored seats. A song about lowriders was once a hit on the radio!

Some Impala owners turn their cars into lowriders! This 1963 Impala is now a lowrider. It has special gold wheels and a very fancy paint job.

TODAY'S IMPALA

In 2000, Chevrolet began making Impalas again! Like the earlier cars, these new Impalas have a lot of nice features and are not too expensive, but they are actually quite different from their ancestors.

The latest Impala is smaller than the huge models Chevrolet made thirty years ago, but it has a roomy, comfortable **interior**. The engine is smaller, but it is more **efficient**, so it does not use a lot of gasoline. The Chevy Impala is still going strong!

Impalas of today are much different from Impalas made in the 1950s and 1960s. This 2000 model is fairly small, and it gets good gas mileage.

MORE TO READ AND VIEW

Books (Nonfiction)   *Chevrolet SS. Muscle Car Color History* (series).
  Robert Genat (Motorbooks International)
Chevy Muscle Cars. Enthusiast Color Series.
  Mike Mueller (Motorbooks International)
Lowriders. Wild Rides (series). Danny Parr, Ann Parr
  (Capstone Press)

Videos (Nonfiction)   *Driving Passion: America's Love Affair with the Car,*
  Part 3 — Golden Age of Detroit. (Turner Home Entertainment)

PLACES TO WRITE AND VISIT

Here are three places to contact for more information:

Alfred P. Sloan Museum
1221 E. Kearsley St.
Flint, MI 48503
USA
1-313-762-1169
www.sloanmuseum.com

**Canadian Automotive
Museum**
99 Simcoe St. South
Oshawa, Ontario L1G 4G7
Canada
1-905-576-1222
**www.city.oshawa.on.ca/
tourism/can_mus.html**

**National Association of
Impala Super Sport Owners**
1565 E. Hwy. 100
Bunnell, FL 32110
USA
1-386-437-3132
www.naisso.net

WEB SITES

Web sites change frequently, but we believe the following web sites are going to last. You can also use good search engines, such as **Yahooligans!** [www.yahooligans.com] or **Google** [www.google.com], to find more information about Chevy Impalas. Here are some keywords to help you: *409 Chevy, Chevrolet, Chevy, Impala, lowriders, muscle cars,* and *Super Sport.*

home.attbi.com/~dkgibson3/impala
The person who hosts this site has a huge 1966 Impala station wagon. Click on different parts of the car to see it from different angles!

popularmechanics.com/automotive/ sub_coll_vintage/1999/12/63_impala
Visit this web site to see many pictures of a Chevy Impala's "409" engine.

woodstock.uplink.net/~mikadink/ impalapage.htm
On this web site, see "before" and "after" photos of a restored 1968 Chevy Impala.

www.angelfire.com/ct2/HOTSHOTS
This web site has a lot of pictures of a beautiful 1958 Chevy Impala convertible!

www.chevrolet.com/impala/index.htm
This is the official web site for Chevrolet. Visit this site to learn all about the latest Impala models.

www.geocities.com/Heartland/Ranch/ 2309/Page3.html
Visit this site to see many pictures of Chevy Impalas from all different years.

www.geocities.com/patriciakreuzer/
The person who hosts this site has restored a 1963 Impala convertible. Visit this site to see pictures of the car being restored.

GLOSSARY

You can find these words on the pages listed. Reading a word in a sentence helps you understand it even better.

accelerate (ak-SELL-er-ate) — go faster 10

Caribbean Sea (cuh-RIB-e-un see) — a part of the Atlantic ocean that is between North and South America 16

convertibles (con-VERT-uh-bulls) — cars with tops that can be folded back or removed for open-air driving 6, 12

custom (KUSS-tum) having special features not found on most models 18

drag strips (DURAG STRIPS) — straight tracks where two cars race each other by accelerating from a complete stop 10

efficient (ef-ISH-unt) — able to do a job without wasting energy 20

hardtops (HARD-tops) — cars that often look like convertibles but have stiff tops that cannot be removed 12

haul (HAWL) — to carry something in a car, truck, or other vehicle 16

horsepower (HORS-pow-ur) — a unit of measurement for an engine's power, based on the amount of work one horse can do 6

insurance (in-SURE-unts) — a contract that guarantees, for a certain amount of money, that something will be fixed or replaced in case of an accident 12

interior (in-TEAR-e-ur) — the inside space of something, such as a house or a car 20

restore (ree-STOR) — to fix something so it seems brand new again 18

sedans (seh-DANZ) — cars that hold four or more people and usually have hard tops that cannot be removed 12

INDEX